Wisdom for the Weary:
Overcoming Life's Obstacles
Vol. 1

Tamara L. Jones

Wisdom for the Weary: Overcoming Life's Obstacles
Copyright © 2017 by Tamara L. Jones

ISBN: 978-0998110332

Published by Semaj Publishing

Printed in the United States of America.

All rights reserved under the International Copyright Law. Contents and/or cover may not reproduced in whole or in part in any form without the express written consent of the Publisher.

This book is available at special discounts for churches, schools, community organizations and educational institutions.

Contact Semaj Publishing
201-243-3700

Author Bookings and Management
lfmanagementgroup@gmail.com

This book is dedicated to those who are tired of being stuck in their past and pain; and ready to be and achieve everything God has for them.

Acknowledgements

To God alone be all the Glory! I am grateful to God for all of the gifts, talents, abilities and opportunities God has and continues to give. Without the Lord's blessing and keeping me I don't know where I would be!

To my mom, Vernell Lucas, thank you for giving me life! Not just through birth but by believing in and pushing me. I love you!

To my God-parents, Gloria Walton and the late Gloria Jones, Mack & Sadie Whitfield; Thank you for introducing me to and helping me cultivate a relationship with God. It is this foundation that started me on this awesome journey. I love you!

To my three awesome daughters, Ganaia, De'Ana, Amanda and my amazing son Divine; Thank you for sharing in this journey with me. Albeit involuntarily lol, you have helped me grow by leaps and bounds through good and bad times. Thank you for sharing me with others, and for always pulling me back and giving me balance in life. Nothing would mean as much to me if it hadn't been for you all. I love you!

To my Right Hand, Vanilla Bean, RLS, Rev. Sissy, 2 Sister-friends- for life and my entire circle of sisters; I appreciate you all more than you know. No matter what stage you entered into my life, you have added value to it!! I love you all!

To my Coach, Dr. Dee C. Marshall; You are the absolute bomb! It is because of You and the deposits you have made in my life that I was able to finally get out of my own way. Thank you, Greatness, for all you do. I love you!

To Robin Devonish, from the very moment we met you saw something in me and immediately pushed and supported me. It is because of you a thought became a vision and a vision became a reality. You are greatly appreciated. I love you!

To Tonya Bryan, My accountability partner and anointed bully. Pancake, what can I say. Thanks for literally kicking me out the box of comfort. I love you!

To LaVon Featherstone, Semaj Publishing and LF Management team- You rock! You are awesome on so many levels. Thank you for taking all of my visions and making them reality. I love you!

To my spiritual father, Pastor B.O. Wilson, my Pastor Darron Thompson, my mentors Pastor Janel York & Rev. Natasha Johnson- Rouse and many more leaders; Thank you each for pouring into me and helping build my foundation. I love you!

To Mr. E. R. - Thank you for simply being you and allowing me to really be me! You inspire me in more ways than you know. I love you!

To my Graphic Designer- Thank you for an amazing cover! You took my minimal thought and made it a great reality! I look forward to working with you in the future. I love you

Table of Contents

Day 1	The Battles of the Righteous!	9
Day 2	Fulfilling Your God Given Dreams	12
Day 3	The Dangers of False Comfort	16
Day 4	Trusting in God!!!	19
Day 5	Forgive and Move on	23
Day 6	Up from the Dust	26
Day 7	Joy in the Midst of Trials	29
Day 8	Down But NOT Out!!!	32
Day 9	Wisdom and Understanding is Key	35
Day 10	Blind Belief	38
Day 11	Healing Comfort	41
Day 12	Once Free, Stay Free	44
Day 13	No Fear Here!!!	47
Day 14	He's Trustworthy	50
Day 15	Are You on Guard??	53
Day 16	Seek Don't Look	56
Day 17	Gifted for His Glory!	59
Day 18	Respond in Faith	62
Day 19	Follow Instructions	65
Day 20	Hope During a Harsh Harvest	68
Day 21	The Best Hiding Place	71
Day 22	Embracing the New You	74

Day 23	Just Relax and Be Ready	77
Day 24	Watch Your Mouth	80
Day 25	God Will Still Do It	83
Day 26	Do You Really Trust Him?	86
Day 27	Learning in Tough Times	89
Day 28	The Reward of Discipline	92
Day 29	Following God with Excitement	95
Day 30	Your Why Will Lead to Your What	98

Day 1

The Battles of the Righteous!
(Romans 5:1-4)

As Christians living in a negatively consuming society we are faced with many trials, temptations, and situations. We all tend to use different scriptures as "spiritual mantras" that help us get through. One such scripture is James 5:16 (NKJV) (the latter portion). "Confess *your* trespasses to one another, and pray for one another, that you may be healed. ***The effective, fervent prayer of a righteous man avails much.***"

Believers hold tight to this one line of scripture as we thank and praise God for healing, deliverance, stability, love, and patience. It gives us the hope to hold on in trying times and comfort in times of despair. Knowing that if we are faithful, obedient and perseverant that our all-sufficient, kind and loving God will hear our prayers and come to our rescue.

Recently, I've found myself holding tight to this as I struggle through various battles in my life. Waiting and looking for relief from the frustration, confusion, and pain of these battles while wondering when will My Father rescue me. Then during my private time with the Lord I presented Him with the question: *Lord, I've been faithful and obedient, and your word says, "the effective and fervent prayer of the righteous man avails much". But it seems like the more I'm faithful and obedient, the less victory seems at hand, and the more battles I am faced with. Why, Lord, Why?*

As I stayed there and waited, and cried, and prayed, and cried some more, The Lord whispered ever so softly to me, "Because the Battles of the Righteous Availeth much!!!"

Initially, I was baffled, shocked and confused all at the same time, because in my natural mind this just did not make any sense to me! But as the day progressed and I asked the Lord to help me understand, He did just that.

He helped me to understand that He uses our various battles; whether with self, the enemy or others to prune and mold us into who and what he has designed and desires for us. It's through these situations that He has our total attention and can mold and shape our character, increase our strengths, develop our integrity, tear down our weaknesses, change our focus, and give us humbleness of spirit!!!

While we should continually be grateful and praise God for the victory and change that occurs because of and through our prayers we should equally be grateful, praise HIM for the victory and change that occurs through our battles.

Wisdom Principle for Today: Don't allow hardships to distract or hinder me, but see them as opportunities to grow.

Notes

Day 2

Fulfilling Your God Given Dreams
(Genesis Chapter 37 - 45)

Growing up as children we all have different dreams and aspirations as to what we want to be when we grow up. Often those dreams are nothing more than glamorized wishes or fantasies, but sometimes unbeknownst to us, God gives us glimpses into our future.

Sadly by the time we reach early adulthood many of those dreams are shattered due to life's circumstances, trials and heartaches. We lose sight of those things that once gave us hope and inspiration, and get caught up in the downward spiral of life's complacencies and routines. As we grow older, we become more and more disheartened as we are sure our opportunity has passed.

But I'm glad to report that this is not so, all is not lost! There is hope and restoration for all that God has promised to you. One of the best examples of this truth is the story of Joseph; God had given him a divine dream, which he would reign over his brothers. In his excitement, he shared this with his brothers who became hateful and jealous. This exchange would be the first of many trials Joseph would face. His brothers plotted to kill him, they sold him into slavery, and his master's wife tried to seduce him. When he refused she lied and he was thrown into jail. He later helped exonerate a wrongly imprisoned butler who promised to help Joseph get freed. Two years after the butler was freed that he remembered Joseph when Pharaoh needed an interpretation of a dream he was given. The butler finally remembered Joseph's interpretation of a dream that freed him. When Pharaoh deemed Joseph's interpretation as acceptable and wise, he began to finalize what God had already put in motion years before. It was almost ten years between the time God gave Joseph the dream and the dream was fulfilled.

What am I saying? Don't allow hope to be stripped from your heart and mind!

Moving forward in life, after a painful past is at best a difficult task. Letting go of years of pain, suffering, accusations, rejection, and betrayal can sometimes seem impossible, but when you place your life in the Hands of the Lord of the Universe, He can make what seems lost and forgotten a bright reality.

In the journey to recovering your God-given dreams there are four things you will actively need to do, to see them accomplished:

1.) *Trust in the LORD with all your heart, And lean not on your own understanding* (Proverbs 3:5 (NKJV)) For if the dreams you possess are truly GOD-Inspired, then only GOD can bring them to pass. Trying to fulfill them on your own will waste your God-given talents, time, tissues, treasures and tongues.

2.) *Don't focus on the amount of time that has passed until your dreams materialize.* Instead, focus on what God has allowed you to accomplish while you wait for your dreams to materialize. Often times God is trying to prepare us for what he has in store for us. But we get caught up in why so much time has passed and questioning why we had to experience so many negative situations that we overlook what he is and has accomplished in us.

3.) *Don't complain, don't worry, don't fret, don't give up, and don't allow your situations and circumstances to dictate to you the outcome of your life.* God has complete control and dominion over the things of this world, and He alone has the final authority of your life!!!
For dominion belongs to the LORD and he rules over the nations. (Psalms 22:28 (NIV))

4.) *Worship God*! The more you keep your mind, heart, spirit, and soul focused on worshipping God the less your circumstances will be in view!!!

Wisdom Principle to Practice: Don't give up! Keep believing, working and pressing to your dreams!

Notes

Day 3

The Dangers of False Comfort
(Psalms 90:17)

Everyone on the face of the earth at some point in life has a time where they set certain goals, dreams, and aspirations. Whether they are personal, family-oriented, work or even ministry these are things we have deep desires for and set out with great passion to complete. We hit the ground running, starting off great with high hopes and enthusiasm. We are organized, disciplined and determined. We plan every aspect of what we feel we need to be successful in this area of our life. Then seemingly out of nowhere, we apply the brakes. We come to a screeching halt and find ourselves stuck in a rut, unsure of how to proceed, wondering how we got so far off the beaten path. We think back to what could have possibly happened that has caused us to be so far of course from our destination.

We think of all the possible culprits; distractions, doubts, and fears. Then we say surely it must have been one of these three things that has veered us of course. Most often this is correct, but there is one culprit we always seem to leave out: THE STATE OF COMFORT!!

During our journey to accomplish our various goals, dreams, and aspirations we get comfortable. Comfortable in our status, comfortable in our thinking, and comfortable in our pursuits.

We get so focused on the end result we envisioned that we lose focus on the work that it must take to get there. We allow what we have already accomplished in these areas to give us a false sense of "arrival" which causes us to stop pursuing these things prematurely. By the time we realize that we haven't actually arrived at the end of our goal we have lost precious time, resources and discouragement begin to settle in.

But don't lose hope, we can get back on track!

First, admit that you have allowed your vision and will to take precedence over the vision and will of God.

Ask God for forgiveness, wisdom, and strength to stay the course as He fulfills His purposes and goals in your life according to HIS will.

Leave your past mistakes and failures where they belong- in the past!!!

Move forward with confidence in who God is, who you are in Him, and what He has called you to do.

Lastly, do spiritual checkpoints with God to make sure you are not going ahead of Him, nor lagging behind Him.

***Wisdom Principle to Practice*:** Don't stay stuck in your comfort zone! Move forward in faith!

Notes

Day 4

Trusting in God!!!
(Proverbs 3:5)

As adults when we think of the word *trust* and how it relates to our relationships, our minds automatically consider a few things:

1.) What has the other person done to earn our trust?
2.) What are the benefits in me trusting them?

We all have the ability to say or do something that *causes* hurt to another person, and we experience situations that are hurtful and damaging to us. These situations leave us cynical, battered, and defensive; severing our ability to trust in man.

When these situations arise, it is absolutely essential that we pray and ask God to heal us from these wounds, to guard our hearts from becoming hard against those who have hurt us, from becoming hard against those who haven't hurt us, and even from becoming hard against HIM. The Word of God admonishes us in Matthew 5:44 (NIV) to "But I tell you, love your enemies and pray for those who persecute you."

When learning to Trust in God, it is important that we do not allow the trust issues that we face with one another to taint our view of who GOD is, why He is deserving of our trust, and why we can't live without trusting in Him. We cannot afford to allow the enemy to use our earthly situations and outcomes as reasons to distrust in God.

Let's look at the above questions and answer them with God in view.

1.) ***What has the other person done to earn our trust?*** We must know that God doesn't have to earn our trust. God is the sovereign ruler of the world and His love for us is unconditional. First of all, God created us in His own image; He gave us life!

Second, while we were yet enemies of God, He sent HIS Only Son, Jesus the Christ, to die for our sins, to give us eternal life, and to reconcile us back into a relationship with God. So again, God doesn't have to do anything to earn our trust, for He has proven to us from the beginning of time His intention and love for us.

2.) ***What are the benefits in me trusting HIM?*** There are so many ways, reasons, and examples but I will sum it up like this because: God has promised in his Word to meet all our needs according to his glorious riches in Christ Jesus. (Philippians 4:19) When we see this scripture many people automatically think of finances, but the scripture does not say God will meet only our financial needs, but all of our needs. That means all of our physical, mental, emotional, spiritual and financial needs. We can Trust in God because the earth is the Lord's and the fullness thereof! "the LORD bestows favor and honor. No good thing does he withhold from those whose uprightly" (Psalms 84:11 (ESV)).

Trusting God requires action and consistency!!! It is more than saying you trust Him when things are well; it means that when you are faced with perilous times and circumstances you look to him for answers. Constant reading and meditating on His Word! Constant prayer and communication with HIM. It will require you to speak the Word of God over yourself, taking action against demonic attacks and thoughts that come against your spirits desire to trust in God.

Trusting in God ultimately means that we completely trust God with all that is in us, our heart, mind, spirit, and soul. Trusting God means not moving ahead of HIM, not staying far behind HIM, not standing still when He says to move, and not moving when He says to stand still.

Wisdom Principle to Practice: Let go of your fears and fully trust in God! You won't regret it!

Notes

Day 5

Forgive and Move on
(Matthew 18:20-22)

Forgiveness is one of the most misunderstood and misused principles of everyday living. Society has taught us to use forgiveness as a tool of retaliation and hostage-taking instead of being used as a tool of healing and restoration.

What is forgiveness? Forgiveness is the willing act of excusing a mistake or offense. That means although the other party may be guilty of committing something harmful or hurtful towards you that you make a conscious effort to free them of the guilt and "penalty" of that offense. Often times we are unable to excuse others, because of the pain attached to the offense. But true forgiveness calls for us to "pardon" the offender. Not that the offense is excusable, as all issues must be dealt with in a godly manner, but you don't hold ill feelings towards the person that committed the act.

Holding on to un-forgiveness creates more problems, issues and hurt than we realize. First, it keeps the offended person hostage emotionally. People carrying un-forgiveness become weighted down with the pain, distrust, and separation that un-forgiveness brings.

Secondly, if we are not careful it begins to seep into other areas of our lives, and we begin to mistreat those who have done no wrong. It also holds the offender hostage, because we tend to try and make the wrongdoer "earn our forgiveness" with a checklist of -if you do this or that, then maybe I will forgive you.

Thirdly, it creates a hindrance in our personal relationship with God and our ability to worship Him freely. Unforgiveness is a tool used by the enemy to keep us in disharmony with one another and with God.

There are two important factors to remember about forgiveness:

First, it is not based on your emotional ability to let go, but your ability to follow what God has given you the ability to do. You are commanded and able to forgive, completely release the pain, frustration, and wrongdoer from the negativity associated with the offense and live in harmony with them.

Secondly, remember that just as someone is in need of forgiveness for hurting you, you too at one point have been and will be in need of forgiveness from someone else. We all, whether intentionally or mistakenly have caused pain to another and must go to them desiring forgiveness and reconciliation with them.

My brothers and sisters, the next time you are hurt and it seems like you are unable to forgive or pardon your offender, ask the Lord to help you to live out His commandment to forgive despite your emotional rationale, and give thanks to HIM for the times He has and will forgive you!

Wisdom Principle to Practice: Learn to forgive others, your freedom is at stake!

Notes

Day 6

Up from the Dust
(Psalm 119:25-28)

Oooweee life has a way of depressing, stressing and distressing even the most faithful and grounded children of God. Oftentimes because of life and circumstances we find ourselves going from the highest high, down to the lowest lows. Don't believe me? Let us look at the psalmist. He went from declaring that the Lord's testimonies were his delight and counselors, to saying his soul clings to the dust. In a blink of an eye, he went from being delighted in the Lord to clingy; being downright attached to the dust in heaviness. Sound familiar? Like the psalmist things occur in our lives that have us up one minute and downright depressed the next. As down as the psalmist seems, he does give us insight as to how we can be restored from this current negative state.

"My soul clings to the dust; Revive me according to Your word." Psalm 119:25 (NKJV) When we are down in the dumps, we must learn to cry out to the Lord and ask Him to revive us with His Word. When we begin to pray and speak the word of God over ourselves and situations it begins to move us from our state of despondency to one of uplifting and encouragement.

The Word of God is the very tool that all believers need and should utilize in overcoming every and anything. Well, you might say I don't really know how to say what I'm feeling or needing, so how can I tell God.

Well, no need to worry; the Holy Spirit residing within

you knows how to make intercession on your behalf. Romans 8:26 (NKJV) says, "Likewise the Spirit also helps in our weaknesses. For we do not know what we should pray for as we ought, but the Spirit Himself makes intercession for us[b] with groanings which cannot be uttered".

"I have declared my ways, and You answered me; Teach me Your statutes." Psalm 119:26 (NKJV) After crying out, we must be willing, determined and receptive to learn and adjust our lives to the will and ways of God. When we learn to make God's ways and statues our standards, we will be able to stand against the lies and attacks of the enemy and the misconceptions of the world and what it teaches.

Finally, after crying out to The Lord, adjusting our lives to the will and ways of God we must then learn to meditate on the very things God reveals to us in His Word. "Make me understand the way of Your precepts; So shall I meditate on Your wonderful works. My soul melts from heaviness; Strengthen me according to Your word." Psalm 119:27-28 (NKJV) The key to being revived is to not meditate on the negativity surrounding you but meditate on the wonderful ways and works of God. For the works of the Lord are immeasurable and His grace is sufficient to sustain us in any situation. God doesn't desire you to cling to the dust in desperation, but He does desire you to cling to HIM in Love, Trust, and Obedience

Wisdom Principle to Practice: In the midst of trying times, cling to who God is and not what you're going through!

Notes

Day 7

Joy in the Midst of Trials
(James 1:2-3)

Growing up I always loved walking around the house singing the songs I heard sung by our choir. One of these songs was "I get joy when I think about what He's done for me". Whenever I heard this song I would just smile, start singing, and just be full of happiness. I thought I had a full understanding of what it meant to be joyful. I thought that life would always be full of happy and joyous moments. What I didn't realize as a child was that there would be times when life's circumstances would hit me like a ton of bricks and that retaining or living in that joy would be strained.

As I grew in age, wisdom, and understanding of whom God was and what was made available to me as His child I began to understand how to identify the great things God was doing in my life and remain joyful. But I also found that real joy doesn't only come through happy moments in life, but real joy can also be experienced in the midst of hard trials.

How is that possible?

You can experience real joy in the midst of trials when you have a true understanding of God's purpose and plan for you and when you know that nothing that happens can change God's course of action for you. The Lord assures us in His Word in Jeremiah 29:11 (NIV) "For I know the plans I have for you," declares the Lord, "plans to prosper you and not to harm you, plans to give you hope and a future." Talk about a reason to be joyful!!!

God has a plan for your life!! That should be reassuring for every child of God that no matter what you face or go through, no matter how hard the trial; your life isn't something that just happened. It's all been planned by the Almighty God! If that isn't assuring enough His Word also teaches in Romans 8:28 (NIV) "And we know that in all things God works for the good of those who love him, who have been called according to his purpose." This knowledge should produce great joy!! As we continue on this journey let's determine to find joy in everything we go through knowing God has a plan, is in control, and that as long as we're in His hands things will always be alright!

Wisdom Principle to Practice: Keep your heart fixed on God's promises, not your problems.

Notes

Day 8

Down but NOT Out!!!
(2 Timothy 1:7)

Life sure does have a way of barreling at us from a myriad of directions. Issue after issue seems to be at our doorstep with no seeming end in sight. We find ourselves in a "Job" position; questioning God on just why He is allowing us to go through all of this turmoil even though we've been faithful and obedient. We feel like surely this season is a mistake, because we have done all God has commanded us to do and that very soon our deliverance will come.

But what do you do when your season of hardship doesn't end when or how you expect it to? What do you do when your circumstances cause you to be bombarded by a number of emotions? How do you overcome what's trying to overpower you?

We must first remember that we don't have to take ownership of everything that we feel! Often times with trials come emotional traps sent by the enemy in the form of depression, frustration, fear, doubt or worry. Although these emotions may present themselves we have the power and authority to deny them and walk in the emotions and mindsets God has given us. For the Word of God says in 2 Timothy 1:7 (NKJV) "For God has not given us a spirit of fear, but of power and of love and of a sound mind". Just because you feel it doesn't mean you have to live it!

Then we must take courage in knowing there is a purpose to this season! Remember that being a child of God does not exempt you from facing hard times James 1:2-3

(NKJV) reminds us; "My brethren, count it all joy when you fall into various trials, knowing that the testing of your faith produces patience". We are encouraged even further in 2 Corinthians 4:8 (NKJV) *"We are* hard-pressed on every side, yet not crushed; *we are* perplexed, but not in despair; persecuted, but not forsaken; struck down, but not destroyed." As a child of God trying times will come but we are to remain joyful because they don't come to harm but to produce Godly characteristics in you so that God's glory may be shown through you. Know that our Father will never allow anything for your destruction!

You may be down for a moment, but with God on your side you will NEVER be out.

Wisdom Principle to Practice*:* Realize that you may be knocked down, but with God on your side you will NEVER BE OUT! Get up and keep going!

Notes

Day 9

Wisdom and Understanding is Key
(*Proverbs 3:13*)

Unhappy with your life? Not content with the direction things are going? Wondering why it seems you know so much, but that information isn't helping you the way you expected? Taking inventory of your life and dissatisfied with what you're finding? Sometimes we get to a place in life where we stop to take stock of our lives only to realize we don't like what we find. Often times it's not that we don't like what we've acquired instead the problem is we've placed too much expectation in what we've acquired.

Many people take time purchasing cars, homes, jewelry and other material possessions to fill the voids in their lives. Others attempt to fill the voids in their lives by obtaining various degrees and becoming knowledgeable in many areas to make themselves seem and feel important. While it's nothing wrong with wanting nice things nor with wanting a great education; these things cannot take precedence over the principle priority of life in having a relationship with God and getting to know Him and ultimately yourself. Proverbs 3:13 (NKJV) says "Happy is the man *who* finds wisdom, and the man *who* gains understanding".

Too often people spend time accumulating what the world deems as worthwhile assets while not spending any time investing in the only thing that counts now and in eternity; your relationship with God. Gaining wisdom means to gain insight, knowledge, discernment, and understanding by experience and through learning. However, the key to wisdom is not how it's obtained but the source it's gained from.

Godly wisdom is imperative for Godly living and is the key to true happiness. When you learn of God's great love for you through His Word and how He has made the greatest sacrifice for you, when you learn that He possesses everything you need and that there's nothing you can't accomplish with Him; when you sit at His feet you gain the wisdom of who He is in totality. Further gaining wisdom of who He is opens the door to you gaining an understanding of everything else life has to offer. You gain understanding of who you are, what you're called to do and how to get there; that leads to not merely being happy but having joy!

Wisdom Principle to Practice: Don't simply learn to know, but learn to Grow!

Notes

Day 10

Blind Belief
(Psalms 27:13)

Many people have come to adopt the popular saying that seeing is believing. They have come to accept this as a viable way of expectation for living not realizing that this very way of thinking is actually robbing them from living fruitful lives. To say seeing is believing is literally saying that you won't believe in what you're waiting for until you can you see it with your own eyes. The greater problem is that while you stand around waiting to see what you're waiting for to manifest, you are constantly being drained of any real hope or faith that it will ever come to pass; because you are already built the mindset that you won't believe it until you see it, and as believers that mindset will zap your strength and your faith.

However, there is an abundant amount of scriptures in the Word that help give hope even when we can't see yet what we are expecting. Psalms 27:13 (NASB) "*I would have despaired* unless I had believed that I would see the goodness of the Lord In the land of the living."

As believers we have to believe that we will see God's grace at work in our lives before it happens. So often we live defeated lives because we operate by what we see currently happening and we get stuck thinking that things will never change for our good.

We allow the negative mentality of this perspective to take root in us and overshadow the faith we possess. But we must always remember that the faith we possess isn't because of the tangible things we see or understand, but because we have built a firm foundation from Romans 8:28(NASB), "And we know that God causes all things to work together for good to those who love God, to those who are called according to *His* purpose." No matter how things look now, no matter how long they've been in that state you must make knowing that God is working an absolute fact in your life.

When God gives you a vision and purpose for your life you must resolve within yourself that even though you can't see how it will work, even though you can't see the clear path and things seem dark, dreary and hopeless; that you won't merely settle for waiting to see before believing rather you will believe even when you can't see.

Wisdom Principle to Practice: Learn to believe what God has said will happen, even when you can't see how it will happen.

Notes

Day 11

Healing Comfort
(2 Corinthians 1:3)

It's sad to say but in 2017 no matter where you go, what you do or experience one thing is sure; this world is hurting! Just turn on the news on any given day and no matter where they are reporting from; whether in a third world country where people are dying of hunger, in communities that have been ravaged by natural storms there is one common denominator exists -hurting people.

You don't even have to look that far; you can look in your own homes and find someone that is hurting- that person may even be you. We face so many trials and circumstances that come up against us that cause a multitude of emotions and reactions that usually only make matters worse. When these issues and emotions are not dealt with they grow and fester; infecting us internally and affecting us externally. You may have been dealt with a series of attacks that the enemy designed to destroy you but there is hope.

First, know that no matter what happens to you God will not allow it to destroy you, instead He will use it to strengthen you. Second, even in the midst of your hurt God will comfort you. It says in 2 Corinthians 1:3(NKJV) "Blessed *be* the God and Father of our Lord Jesus Christ, the Father of mercies and God of all comfort". We have the assurance of first knowing that our heavenly father is the God of ALL comfort. Meaning no matter what you've gone through, He has the power and ability to comfort you in the midst of the most trying times. But even more comforting is that the same comfort He gives us that He empowers and enables us to share in comforting others.

2 Corinthians 1:4 (NKJV) goes on to say: "who comforts us in all our tribulation that we may be able to comfort those who are in any trouble, with the comfort with which we ourselves are comforted by God."

You see the comfort and healing we received is not just for us to hold onto, but once we are whole we are to go back and comfort those who are still hurting so that they may experience the love and healing power of God. So that others can be freed from the bondage that entangles them, and live the whole and productive lives God designed for them.

Wisdom Principle to Practice: Allow God to heal you, so He can use you to heal others!

Notes

Day 12

Once Free, Stay Free
(Galatians 5:1)

At the age of 17, Michael Smith was wrongly accused of second-degree murder and was sentenced to 15 years to life. While in prison he fervently fought for his freedom all the while maintaining his innocence. Then after ten long years of fighting, and appeals, prayers and waiting Michael got the break he needed. New evidence was discovered that would eventually exonerate Michael and set him free. After ten long years, Michael would finally be able to go home to his family a free man and free from the guilt of what he was accused of; completely free. After just a few months of being home things didn't seem right. Michael seemed distant and confused; he no longer seemed happy to be home and seemed to be stuck in a rut. He seemed to spiral down, became depressed and retreated within himself. Then without warning the unimaginable happened, Michael committed a violent burglary and was sent back to prison. When it was time for his sentencing the judge asked Michael, "Why after all of these years of fighting for your freedom, maintaining your innocence and finally being exonerated would you commit such a heinous crime knowing you would end up here?" Michael's response? "I just couldn't believe I was actually free and I couldn't handle the new life that came with my freedom, so I decided it would be best for me to go back to what I know".

As hard as it is to believe this fictitious story and how someone would choose imprisonment over freedom, many of us do this very thing in the spiritual. We pray and ask

God for deliverance over an issue, addiction or problem, but often have a hard time maintaining our freedom. Receiving freedom in God and from God may not cost us anything, but maintaining our freedom will require obedience and sacrifice on our part

Even if you have grappled with strongholds for years, once God sets you free stay free. Once you are forgiven and set free you don't have to sit back and believe the taunts of the enemy; that will draw you back into his grips. But you must constantly submit yourself to God and work at protecting your thoughts as it says in Romans 12:2a (NKJV), "And do not be conformed to this world, but be transformed by the renewing of your mind".

Don't believe the negativity of the world or the whispers of the enemy that says you could never be free. But remember the words in John 8:36 (NKJV), "Therefore if the Son makes you free, you shall be free indeed." Once Jesus sets you free you have the capacity to walk in complete freedom.

Wisdom Principle to Practice: Do the work in maintaining your freedom in God and watch how God changes your life.

Notes

Day 13

No Fear Here!!!
(2 Timothy 1:7)

Ever find yourself in a situation where you're constantly thinking and worried about the outcome of the situation? You contemplate how the current status of a situation and its pending outcome will affect you now and later. You sit and think, and think, and think until it feels like your mind is going to explode from the weight of all the thinking. You allow your emotions to take you to a place where uncertainty and fear reign in your thought life and actions, and you seem to get to a place where you feel shaken to your core.

If you've been in this place or even if you are there now, don't despair or beat yourself up. Many believers have found themselves at this crossroad where fear seemingly outweighs their faith, but there is a great hope! Although we all may have unwillingly reached this place of fear and uncertainty at one point or another, our God is right there to guide us back to a place of peace, trust and strength. However in order to get there we must first know what God has said about fear and faith and be willing to apply it to our lives with our whole being.

We must denounce the worldly teaching about the state of fear. Contrary to popular belief fear is not a natural response for a child of God! The Word says in 2 Timothy 1:7 (NKJV) "For God has not given us a spirit of fear, but of power and of love and of a sound mind." Fear is not a natural emotion that God has given His people; it is a device of the enemy to keep us bound. Understand there is a great difference between being godly cautious and being fearful. Being Godly cautious implores one to use godly wisdom before moving, ensuring they are following the voice of God. Being fearful keeps one bound from making any movement or decisions out of what is seen in the natural.

Listen, whenever you desire to do what God has ordained for your life; fear will always present itself. Why? Well, because oftentimes God will tell you to move without revealing all of the steps prior to your moving. Therefore stepping out of your comfort zone and into faith can be a scary thing, but we must still move. Not only that, but the enemy does not want to see you walk or achieve what God has for you, so he will bombard you with thoughts of why it can't be done by you. But as quickly as he hurls those thoughts at you, you must be just as quick at denouncing them. Declare victory now, knowing that just because you feel it doesn't mean you have to keep it.

Wisdom Principle to Practice: Pray and ask God for discernment between fear and godly wisdom. Once you realize what's present move accordingly, denounce fear and walk in wisdom!

Notes

Day 14

He's Trustworthy
(Provers 3:5-6)

Many people walk around looking for validation from others, opening themselves up to people in hopes that they would be trustworthy with their hearts and lives. Unfortunately, more often than not these people are let down because the ones they entrusted themselves to did nothing to garner such an honor nor did they give any assurance that trusting in them would reap any benefits.

When one is given the responsibility of caring for someone who trusts them, many regretfully take advantage of that person's vulnerability and hurt them instead of helping them. Gratefully as believers the same doesn't ring true for our relationship with God. However, as believers we have to be mindful not to taint our view of God's trustworthiness with the brush of hurt we have because of how someone has let us down or broken our trust.

When making the choice to trust in God you never have to worry or consider that your trust in Him will end up hurting or damaging you in any way. First, He has already proven his love and desire for you by giving you the best gift you could ever receive. John 3:16 (NKVJ) says "For God so loved the world that He gave His only begotten Son, that whoever believes in Him should not perish but have everlasting life". We are reminded further of his love in Romans 5:8 (NKJV), "But God demonstrates His own love toward us, in that while we were still sinners, Christ died for us".

Not only do we see how much He loved us even before we loved Him but we also have assurances of what trusting Him will bring Proverbs 3:5-6 (NKJV) reminds us, "Trust in the Lord with all your heart, And lean not on your own understanding; In all your ways acknowledge Him, And He shall direct your paths". Trusting in God not only gives us peace, security and hope but it also leads to clear direction for your life.

We are able to talk, walk, trust in, and follow after God because Christ made it possible.

When I think of summing up our ability to trust in God I'm reminded of the song writer who penned this well-known gospel song:

Tis so sweet to trust in Jesus,
Just to take Him at His word;
Just to rest upon His promise;
Just to know, Thus saith The Lord

Wisdom Principle to Practice: When you are tempted to ask God to show you why He can be trusted simply look in the mirror.

Notes

Day 15
Are You on Guard??
(Proverbs 4:23)

Throughout the course of a day we are all bombarded by a barrage of thoughts that can seemingly overwhelm us. Family issues, bills, overwhelming workload, missed dreams, past hurts, broken relationships and future hopes. Not only can these thoughts overwhelm us, but if we're not mindful of their presence and careful of their power we can find ourselves led into a myriad of emotions and actions we never intended to feel or do.

Many people find themselves in places and situations all because they've failed to stay on guard. Proverbs 4:23 (NKJV) says "Keep your heart with all diligence, For out of it *spring* the issues of life." So many people spend a considerable amount of time guarding worldly possessions and things that they have high regard for, but leave the most important parts of their being unguarded.

Consider for a moment, what do you possess more vital and valuable than your mind and heart? What could possibly hold more value to you than the two things that have the ability to drive your every action? Let me just make it clear; nothing you ever inherit, purchase or find will be more important or worthy of guarding than your mind and heart. Why? Because the success to living begins with the mind and heart; and if we're not careful the pattern can lead us to a destructive end.

What in the world does the success to living look like and how does it work? Well, in an unguarded life the success looks like this; negative thoughts lead to damaging emotions, damaging emotions lead to unwise actions and unwise actions lead to consequences. Don't believe me? We'll think of a time in your life where you found yourself dealing with severe consequences that either came very close to or may have destroyed a part of your life. I'm pretty sure if you trace your steps back to how you started on that destructive path it will lead you to some unguarded thoughts and feelings.

Likewise, think about a time in your life where you had the enjoyment of fulfilling a goal or watching the fruit of wise decisions unfold in your life. When you stop and recall how you got to these great results you will find that you had specific thoughts in your mind; positive thoughts lead to a surrendered life, a surrendered life leads to God-led actions, God-led actions that lead to fruitful and proper actions.

Want to live a purposeful life; I admonish you to stay on guard over what's really important!

Wisdom Principle to Practice: Be intentional and mindful in keeping healthy boundaries!

Notes

Day 16

Seek Don't Look
(Matthew 6:33)

In 1980, Johnny Lee sang the title track for Urban Cowboys that became a very popular song both lyrically and comically. 'Lookin' For Love' became a popular song that was not only redone but was even done as a comedy skit on Saturday Night Live. The line, "lookin for love in all the wrong places", became a running joke amongst friends who suffered poor relationships and used as the excuse.

But if we were to take a longer and deeper look at this line, we will sadly find that this line shines light as to why so many people live such despondent and hopeless lives. Looking for love in all the wrong places is a true-life statement that has misled, damaged and confused people and left them in a place where they don't know who they are or what they can have. Many people wind up looking for love due to a myriad of circumstances. Maybe they were abandoned as a child by both parents, maybe they were abused by someone they loved, maybe they had many people around them, but no one ever affirmed who they were. All of these scenarios could leave a person void and looking for love but in all the wrong places.

Places like alcoholic beverages, gangs or abusive relationships, places like immoral or illicit relationships, or simply places that leave them emotionally, spiritually and mentally bankrupt. Places that leave them helpless, hopeless, despondent and discouraged feeling like there is no hope for them. All because they are looking for love, acceptance and purpose in things and people that were not designed to provide it for them. They may have begun looking in the wrong places, but praise God they have the opportunity to turn it around.

How?

The step towards joy, peace, wholeness and purpose is to Seek God First!! In Matthew 6:33 (NKJV) we find Jesus preaching on the topic and advises us not to worry. He says, "But seek first the kingdom of God and His righteousness, and all these things shall be added to you". At the time He was discussing the external needs of man, but we serve a savior who came to meet ALL of our needs! He tells us don't worry God know what you need in every area but you must seek Him first!

Believe that God not only has the ability to meet all of your external needs but even those internal needs! The need for love, peace, and real joy. All of these things can be experienced when you SEEK a relationship with God, and not LOOK for others to fill a void they were not ordained to fill. The truth of the matter is, only your Creator can fill the voids in your life.

Wisdom Principle to Practice: Take back the power and permission you've given others to fill and/or validate you.

Notes

Day 17

Gifted for His Glory!
(1 Corinthians 12:11)

What do you know how to do? What are you passionate about? Are you good at it? Know someone in the same field as you? Feel threatened? Well, you shouldn't!

All of us have been given gifts, talents and abilities that have the dual purpose of glorifying God and edifying each other. But too often we become envious of others when we see they have the same or similar gifts and talents as us. However, we have no right to get territorial about the gifts we have because we did nothing to receive them. 1 Corinthians 12:11(NKJV) says, "But one and the same Spirit works all these things, distributing to each one individually as He wills". No one has the right to feel negative towards another person because they feel someone else walks in their God-given gifts better than they do. Nor do we have to feel inadequate about the gifts God has given us because the truth is there is no such thing as a "lesser gift".

People make the mistake of becoming personal managers over their gifts, thinking they can do whatever they want because they own that right. Instead, they need to come to the understanding that these gifts are not something you work hard to get because they are not yours but God's. However, while we can't work to get them, we must work hard to maintain them as stewards for God. We have been entrusted by God with these gifts to bring Him glory and help others, that's it! They are not given for self-gain, however when we are faithful God will allow the fruit of your stewardship to bless you.

There's yet another reason we don't have to be envious of anyone else's gifts; Proverbs 18:16 (NKJV) teaches us, "A man's gift makes room for him, And brings him before great men." You never have to worry that there will be no use for your gifts because another person is operating in it. The word says a man's gift will make room for them, meaning that each person's gifting will make room for them. It does not say we have to compete, worry or diminish another person for what God has called them to do. Everything about you your gifts, talents, abilities, personality and purpose have been given to you to reach certain people. The truth is that "everything isn't for everybody". Meaning that God knew exactly the type of people He would need you to touch with your life. That's why you don't have to worry about what someone else is doing.

As each person remains faithful, obedient, and disciplined working in their area of gifting, talents and abilities God will make sure opportunities will open up specifically designed for them. Our gifts, even if similar, are given to complement each other as we work in the kingdom to glorify God!

Wisdom Principle to Practice: Walk authentically in who God created you to be and what He has gifted you to do and let him work out the rest.

Notes

Day 18

Respond in Faith
(Matthew 14:28-31)

"Peter said to Him, "Lord, if it is you, command me to come to You on the water." And He said, "Come!" And Peter got out of the boat, and walked on the water and came toward Jesus. But seeing the wind, he became frightened, and beginning to sink, he cried out, "Lord, save me!" Immediately Jesus stretched out His hand and took hold of him, and said to him, "You of little faith, why did you doubt?" (Matthew 14:28-31 NASB)

How many times have you and I asked God for a sign for his presence? Some inclination that the little voice we heard was Him? We declare God I will do whatever you tell me to do, whenever you tell me. We start off with so much fire and determination but more often than we care to admit we have Peter moments.

Peter was in the boat trying to find comfort in the midst of the storm and saw Jesus afar off. Peter grappled with whether or not the presence he saw on the water was the Master or a ghost. Being unsure he made this petition for a sign; *Lord if it is you command me to come*. Peter specifically asked Jesus to confirm His presence by a specific request but when He did Peter did not respond in the same faith he previously petitioned Jesus. When Jesus commanded him to come, Peter initially stepped out on faith, started moving forward toward Jesus but then got distracted but what he saw and felt and began to sink into the water.

Many of us are like Peter we petition God with full trust asking Him to move but when he does our response doesn't match our request. When you stand in faith and ask The Lord for what you need, don't allow the circumstances of your life overwhelm you and distract you from the Master's voice.

Like Peter. God is commanding us to manifest things in our lives but we must stand steadfast in trusting Him despite what we feel or how things seem. We must learn to follow His voice no matter what or face the same fate as Peter, and begin to sink in the things God gave us the power to work on. Know when you respond in faith God will supernaturally make things work on your behalf; for your good and His glory!

Wisdom Principle to Practice: Don't allow distractions to take you of course! Once you take that first step keep moving!

Notes

Day 19

Follow Instructions
(Proverbs 4:10-13)

There are many times in life where we choose to hold on to the advice of others. Loved ones, trusted friends, and motivational speakers all because we believe their words will provide for us what we are looking for.

While the encouragement of others has its place, we often fail to put it into place. We make the mistake of placing all our value in what they have to say while neglecting to put any value in what God has to say. We assume because they have been in similar situations that they know best or we feel what worked for them will also work for us. Sometimes we find ourselves in sticky situations because we have not sought the counsel of God before seeking the counsel of man.

But who knows what's best for us better than God? Who can give us better direction than God? No one! No matter how well intending people are and how much wisdom they have, no one can give us better words for our lives. No one can provide any promises with their instructions other than God. Now, I know what you may be saying, "I've read the word, I've heard what God has said but it doesn't seem to be working". Well, I have a question, "What are you doing while you're listening and waiting?"

Proverbs 4:10-13 (NKJV) says, "Hear, my son, and receive my sayings, And the years of your life will be many. I have taught you in the way of wisdom; I have led you in right paths. When you walk, your steps will not be hindered, And when you run, you will not stumble. Take firm hold of instruction, do not let go; Keep her, for *she is* your life."

How do we respond properly to His instructions?

First, receive His instructions. He will protect us as we follow Him. He says because He has taught us wisdom and leads us on the right path our steps will be not be hindered, we will be able to move forward without any blockage. Further we can run knowing we can move forward swiftly, full steam ahead and not worry about falling.

Second, take firm hold and don't let go! We must fully embrace that God's Word contains everything we need to make it through this journey! Once we embrace that we must hold on to His Word for dear life.

Wisdom Principle to Practice: Once God gives you instructions, follow them as is. Know all that is required is your obedience and knowing that God is responsible for the outcome.

Notes

Day 20

Hope During a Harsh Harvest
(Galatians 6:7-9)

"Be not deceived; God is not mocked: for whatsoever a man soweth, that shall he also reap. For he that soweth to his flesh shall of the flesh reap corruption; but he that soweth to the Spirit shall of the Spirit reap life everlasting. And let us not be weary in well doing: for in due season we shall reap, if we faint not." Galatians 6:7-9 (KJV)

Many times we read this scripture with great excitement because we focus on the latter "good" of the scripture. The parts that read, "but he that soweth to the Spirit shall of the Spirit reap life everlasting life. And let us not be weary in well doing; for in due season we shall reap, if we faint not". While this should incite a level of encouragement and excitement concerning the anticipation of reaping the harvest of the goodness sown, how do you address or anticipate the beginning portion of the scripture? The portion that says," Be not deceived; God is not mocked: for whatsoever a man soweth, that shall he also reap. For he that soweth to his flesh shall of the flesh reap corruption." The law of reaping and sowing states that whatever we have intentionally spent time sowing (investing in) that is what we shall reap (receive back), that seems all well and fine when it's on the positive end; but what do we do when our season of harvesting comes around and it's a season of a harsh harvest.

As we journey through life we tend to gravitate toward the parts of the bible that "make us feel better", but the goal of the bible is for us to learn how to **BE** better, not just feel better. The truth of reality is, we do not always live pleasing unto God, there are times we sow out of our flesh things God never intended. Although we may face the consequences of a harsh harvest due to our actions, as the scripture reminds us, we do not have to lose heart nor fear this time of harvest because despite the reason of this harsh Harvest God loves us so that He doesn't allow us to suffer long.

1 Peter 5:10 (NIV) says, "And the God of all grace, who called you to his eternal glory in Christ, after you have suffered a little while, will himself restore you and make you strong, firm and steadfast".

Listen, even if you're in a season of dealing with the consequences of past sin know that there's hope in and joy after the harsh harvest!

Know that if you repent of your sins and make the conscious choice to live a life pleasing to God that He will not leave you alone to suffer, nor will He allow the enemy or anyone else to condemn you. Receive and walk in His forgiveness knowing that when you decide to live authentically and righteously before Him, He will be pleased with you.

Hold onto to the hope that as a loving Father He will allow his grace to carry you through this season; and in due time, His mercy to carry you out of this season.

Wisdom Principle to Practice: Don't allow the mistakes of your past to keep you downtrodden. Know that even in the midst of dealing with your consequences that God loves and cares about you.

Notes

Day 21

The Best Hiding Place
(Psalms 119:14)

Sometimes the circumstances of life can weigh you down beyond anything you ever imagined. It seems like issue after issue arises; you deal with one major thing then bam here comes another. Before you can rejoice that you got through one problem you are hit with another. You wonder what in the world is going on? You pray and cry out to God wondering where He is at such a time, wondering if just maybe He has put too much on you.

You sit and ponder your options and then almost suddenly that ole enemy presents you with a slew of options, that appeal to your flesh but hide the damage they really contain. The enemy strategically plans, plots and waits for us to get to our lowest point to present his best and most treacherous options to us if we are not careful, mindful and deliberate we wind up choosing them, because we only see what's on the surface of his "gifted options". *What do they look like?* Well, the enemy always dresses up his destructive options to trap us. One option may be your favorite wine or "adult" beverage that under "non" stressful times you enjoy on occasion; but in this time of frustration he may whisper "drink a little more, drown out the pain it's alright; it's only one time". But what he doesn't tell you is that one time of self-medication can lead you down a path of unimaginable destruction because the taste will be so comforting that you'll look to it again.

Another option could be the soothing arms of someone God did not ordain for you. The enemy will whisper,

"Relax that standard a little bit. It's ok to give yourself to them; nothing's going to happen. Look at everyone else that has done it; nothing happened to them. What he doesn't tell you is the long-term effects sexual sins have on you mentally and physically amongst other things.

We must truly know and understand that there is nothing and no one that can really cover or comfort us the way God does. While he is a cunning adversary, we can reject his options. *How?* By determining our source of strength before seasons of hardship occur. Psalms 119:114 (NKJV) declares, "You *are* my hiding place and my shield; I hope in Your word". You must know and believe that in God you have the best hiding place! *Why?* Because when you hide in Him who has come to save, heal and set you free; there is no complete protection, perfect peace and unadulterated truth that will never lead you astray

Wisdom Principal to Practice: In times of struggle do not turn to substances or people to hide from your problems, turn to God to help you with your problems.

Notes

Day 22

Embracing the New You
(2 Corinthians 5:17)

As a society, we have come to rely on various statements and catchphrases to either express how we feel or to defend ourselves or our position in a situation. One of these statements is, "That's just how I am", which is usually used after we have offended someone and refuse to take responsibility for our actions. This statement is extremely detrimental as we use it to let ourselves off the hook from changing the offensive behavior or worse than that as believers when we utter these words we are also limiting the power of God from moving in our lives. We are not exhibiting faith in God's word that teaches us in 2 Corinthians 5:17 (NASB), "Therefore if anyone is in Christ, *he* is a new creature; the old things passed away; behold, new things have come.".

When you and I accept Christ as Savior, we accept the fact that Christ has come to save us from the penalty of sin (which is death) because He has died for the sins of mankind. But when we accept Christ as Lord we accept the power of His salvific work that has the ability to change (sanctify) us in our daily living. Becoming a new creature does not mean we receive new bodies but we do receive new instructions and directions as to what to do and say with the bodies we have. When we accept Christ we now have possibility and responsibility to allow ourselves to be purged of the worldly ways we've become accustomed to living and begin living the way God intended but we must be willing! Being willing to allow God to change us can only occur when we recognize we don't have to live by the principles and precepts we've picked up in the world and by learning to live a surrendered life to God and not living a surrendered life to self. Many people falsely believe that living surrendered to God is an unachievable task but that's not the case Psalms 37:7(a) (GW) reminds us; "Surrender yourself to the Lord, and wait patiently for him."

We must learn that becoming a new creature requires our full surrender of self and patience in God's process of changing us. Being remade is not an overnight process however when you allow God to work in and through you the process will manifest in your life. You will no longer say, "that is just who I am", but you'll begin to say, "Praise God I'm not who I used to be".

Wisdom Principle to Practice: Don't make excuses for your behaviors! Make adjustments to your behaviors!

Notes

Day 23

Just Relax and Be Ready
(James 1:2)

We often face temptations, trials, hardships and setbacks that catch us by surprise, but truthfully they shouldn't. As believers we have become complacent and careless in being prepared for these times, because we have adopted a fierce mentality for prosperity and "happy" times. We've allowed ourselves to constantly be on the lookout for our seasons of blessings that we leave ourselves unprepared for seasons of hardships. While as the children of God we should look for blessings but we should also expect hard times to occur in our lives. Why? Because in James 1:2 (NKJV) we are reminded "My brethren, count it all joy when you fall into various trials", The latter portion of this scripture says, "when you fall into various trials," this tells us these seasons of hardships are inevitable.

So then why are we often shaken when they show up? Why are we rocked to our core as if we are totally out of the loop from their presence? Because we've allowed ourselves to adopt a "that won't happen to me" mindset. *But the real question is, why not you?* I Corinthians 10:13 (NKJV) tells us, "No temptation has overtaken you except such as *is* common to man; but God *is* faithful, who will not allow you to be tempted beyond what you are able, but with the temptation will also make the way of escape, that you may be able to bear *it*."

NEWSFLASH: These types of hardships are common to mankind and guess what that includes you! So how do you prepare for these times? Well let's look at a few things:

First, stop thinking you're immune to hardships. Expect and accept that things are bound to happen. But that God is going to bring you through them triumphantly!

Second, know that what's happening to you has happened to others. What you are facing isn't some unknown phenomenon. You'll make it just as they have.

Third, God loves you so much that He will not allow you to deal with anything above your capacity to handle. Although it may seem rough, know that you've already been equipped to handle it.

Lastly, don't give in under pressure. Know that God planned your escape route, before the season even started. God doesn't wait to see how you're going to handle it, to decide how to get you out. The season comes with the exit plan, but you have to persevere through the process to get to the end.

Wisdom Principle to Practice: Don't be surprised by hard times. Be prepared for them.

Notes

Day 24

Watch Your Mouth
(Ephesians 4:29)

Are you mindful of what you say before you say it? Do you consider the impact your words will have when they land in the ears of others? Do you stop to think about the influence your words have? More often than not people speak various things to, about and at others without any real understanding of how their words touch the lives of others. The world teaches the principle of speak your mind so you can be heard but The Word of God teaches the contrary. The word says in Ephesians 4:29 (NKJV), "Let no corrupt word proceed out of your mouth, but what is good for necessary edification, that it may impart grace to the hearers".

The word corrupt can be boiled down to one word: evil. The bible teaches us not to speak words of evil to one another but words that edify and bring life. Many often quote Proverbs 18:21 (NKJV) when it comes to their personal life where it states, "Death and life are in the power of the tongue, and those who love it will eat its fruit". But they mistakenly leave this declaration with a one-sided view. While we should be mindful to speak life and not death over our own lives, we must be equally mindful and concerned to speak in the same manner over others. The word has given the command and responsibility to us to watch what we say. Now you may be thinking that this is just a little too hard for you to maintain on a constant basis. You may be thinking, well you don't know how I get when I'm angry or that you don't know how to even get it under control. Well, one sure fire way to watch what comes out your mouth is to watch what goes into your mind.

Philippians 4:8(NKJV) says, "Finally, brethren, whatever things *are* true, whatever things *are* noble, whatever things *are* just, whatever things *are* pure, whatever things *are* lovely, whatever things *are* of good report, if there *is* any virtue and if *there is* anything praiseworthy—meditate on these things." When you begin meditating on these things it will decrease the possibility of anything evil coming out. The more good you deposit in the more good will come out. Sometimes our obstacles are not always external, but internal battles concerning our character and behavior. Battles we have to fight to win!

What's the goal to guarding and watching, you ask? Simple that the hearer may receive an abundant amount of grace and that God your father is pleased with you!

***Wisdom Principle to Practice*:** Before you speak it, make sure it's truth not just your feelings, that it helps the listener and glorifies God.

Notes

Day 25

God Will Still Do It
(Numbers 23:19)

As children our parents do their best to encourage us to set goals for our lives. They ask us what our passions are and do their best to help cultivate them. As we grow up and attend school our teachers join the team trying to guide us on the right path for our lives. As we come to know God in our own personal relationships our Christian leaders come aboard to further encourage us to become who God has designed us to be. While a lot of people experience this healthy system of guidance, the truth is that not everyone does. Leaving many to fight and fend for themselves merely tumbling through life trying to find their niche. Many know within themselves what God has spoken to them, but because of the lack of guidance in the natural they fail to see the possibility of it manifesting.

Those without proper guidance do find their way but usually after many hardships and failures. They experience hurt and betrayal from those they love and trust, and come to a place of giving up on others and themselves. They determine within their hearts that they will never trust another and that the dreams they had our long gone. Because they have suffered along the way their mindset usually places them in a state of distrust and hesitance in letting others in. While their hesitance is understandable their tendency to equate these feelings to God is not.

We also cannot allow past mistakes, decisions or failures to rob us of the hopes or desires of what's ahead of us!

What we must understand is that no matter what we experience with others on our journey to fulfilling our life's plan that we should never hold God hostage with our emotions because of other sinful fallen men. First off, "God is not a man that He should lie." Numbers 23:19 (NASB) No matter how long ago God made a promise to you, HE WILL complete it in you until it is accomplished!

Just like He promised the children of Israel in Genesis 28:15(NASB) "Behold, I am with you and will keep you wherever you go, and will bring you back to this land; for I will not leave you until I have done what I have promised you." We must know without a shadow of a doubt that God is always with and for us, even when we stray. The children of Israel strayed in the sight of God, yet He fulfilled His promise to them, albeit with latter generations, but He never went back on His promise.

Know that even if you stray off course but you repent and be determined to get back on track; God is still with you and guiding you. Just like God kept His promise to them, He will do the same for you.

***Wisdom Principle to Practice*:** Don't allow time, issues or past failures to keep you from what God has for you!

Notes

Day 26

Do You Really Trust Him?
(Matthew 8:25-26)

"Then His disciples came to *Him* and awoke Him, saying, "Lord, save us! We are perishing!" But He said to them, "Why are you fearful, O you of little faith?" Then He arose and rebuked the winds and the sea, and there was a great calm." Matthew 8:25-26 (NKJV)

In Matthew 8 we find Jesus descending from the mountain after delivering the "Sermon on the Mount" where He delivered many life-giving messages to the people. After delivering these messages Jesus descended the mountain with disciples in tow and began ministering various miracles and healings. While Jesus was ministering, the disciples were watching how great and powerful their Messiah was. One would think that while they watched their faith would be increasing, their trust would be building and their fear would be dissipating. However, we find that's not the case.

Soon after Jesus and His disciples entered a boat they found themselves in a great storm. The storm was so fierce that the bible says the waves covered the boat. It would appear as though this storm was so bad that the boat seemed like it would capsize. The disciples became so fearful that they ran to Jesus asking Him to save them. *Sounds familiar?* There are times in our lives that circumstances occur suddenly and fiercely, overwhelming us beyond compare and we run to God crying out save me, save me. Now that might seem like a natural response but as children of God, should it be? For those that have been walking and communing with God, should our first response be that of despair? Absolutely not! While it is a natural response in our flesh to run for safety, as Believers who have seen God work miracles in our lives and the lives of others it is not the kind of faith response God desires, nor does it build our witness or edify others.

Contrary to how things seem we must always believe that God knew about the storm before we got into it, has the power to control the storm once we are in it, and the ability to bring us out of it. The truth of the matter is we cannot proclaim faith in God yet respond in fear when our circumstances bear down on us.

Remember the God you serve has the power to control and quiet both; you and your storm

Wisdom Principle to Practice: When life begins to barrel at you, don't respond in fear or your flesh, respond in faith!

Notes

Day 27

Learning in Tough Times
(Hebrews 5:7-8)

"Who, in the days of His flesh, when He had offered up prayers and supplications, with vehement cries and tears to Him who was able to save Him from death, and was heard because of His godly fear, though He was a Son, *yet* He learned obedience by the things which He suffered." Hebrews 5:7-8 (NKJV)

So many Christians constantly profess the desire to manifest a godly character but few ever want to go through the process of godly character being produced in them. Sadly, the world's precepts of having things easily given or attained in life have crept its way into the church, rendering many incapable of growing in full spiritual maturity because they are looking for the easy way out. But when it comes to developing godly character there is no such thing as easy growth.

In this day and age many Christians are stuck in a place of stagnant growth because they want to be accepted the way they are by others and by God. But God never desires to leave us the way He finds us. Romans 8:29 (NASB) says, "For those whom He foreknew, He also predestined to *become* conformed to the image of His Son, so that He would be the firstborn among many brethren". God desires for each one of His children to be re-imaged into the image of His Son, which would manifest godly character in us as we begin manifesting the qualities of Christ in our lives. Developing Christian character is a lifelong process that we undertake once we profess Christ as Lord and Savior.

It's a process that we must willingly undertake and go through in God's timing and in God's ways. It's a process that God desires for each of His children way before we were even born. It's a process we must understand will come with seasons of suffering.

The problem we face in learning the lessons and developing the character God is trying to develop in us; is that we want to rush the development process or we want to dictate to God what we want Him to use to develop us. We want to experience maximum growth and power with minimal effort, pain or suffering.

We cannot only desire and choose to grow through positive situations or circumstances. But we must be willing to grow through and in everything we experience.

When we find ourselves in seasons of struggle or suffering don't simply cry, pray or petition your way out but realize what you're going through is designed to grow you for His glory.

Wisdom Principle to Practice: Don't despise or denounce the lessons in your hard times, but look at everything as an opportunity to grow!

Notes

Day 28

The Reward of Discipline
(Hebrews 12:11)

"All discipline for the moment seems not to be joyful, but sorrowful; yet to those who have been trained by it, afterwards it yields the peaceful fruit of righteousness." Hebrews 12:11(NASB)

Say the word *discipline* in a crowded room and you will likely receive a response of cringe-worthy looks and deep sighs. When people hear or think of the word *discipline* they automatically think of all the negative connotations that have been associated with it. Whether you think about the physical discipline in fitness training, the discipline of an unruly child or the discipline of studying for school; saying the word discipline seems to bring with it a cloud of discomfort.

Yet the word teaches us that while discipline brings discomfort for the moment, if you stick with it the rewards it yields is worth the training it provides. So what holds us back from the benefits of discipline? One thing, our focus. Many falsely believe that the discomfort we face when disciplining ourselves is what holds us back, but this is not the truth. The fact that we focus on the discomfort we feel is what actually holds us back. The fact of the matter is discomfort is to be expected in any manner of discipline we enact in our lives. If you're trying to lose weight, then you should expect the discomfort of removing certain foods and beginning a workout regimen. If you have a strict study regimen you will feel the discomfort of missing certain pleasures in order to have sufficient time to study. If you're trying to increase your intimacy with God you should expect resistance in your flesh. Discomfort will always be present when you determine to change your life.

When we embrace the fact that discomfort is inevitable and temporary, we will find the strength to endure it and persevere to our goals. When you discipline your eating and fitness habits you will have a healthier temple. When you maintain proper study habits you will possess the degree you work so hard for. When you discipline your flesh you will receive the reward of God's peace and the manifestation of righteousness will unfold in your life. Don't shy away from or avoid the necessary disciplines in your life. Instead embrace it, learn from it then sit back and enjoy its rewards

Wisdom Principles to Practice: Make discipline your friend, not your enemy!

Notes

Day 29

Following God with Excitement
(Isaiah 49:17)

When I was a little girl there was nothing more enjoyable than being able to spend countless hours outside with my friends. There were many games we enjoyed but a few of my favorites were- *Mother May I, Simon Says, Red Light/Green Light.* There was something in the excitement of waiting for the leader to give instruction and trying my best to meet their expectations and to receive their approval and winning the game.

Now that I'm older and on this Christian journey I've learned I have to have that same excitement now in following God. Every day I wait with joyous anticipation as to how I can serve Him and follow His instructions. Now my waiting is not because I think I'll do a great job in doing everything that He says, contrary to that, I already know that I will fail Him at some point throughout the day. Yet I wait with joy because I know regardless of my failures His directions and guidance will never lead me astray nor will he abandon me.

Why be excited? Because God desires that I be profitable as His child.

Isaiah 48:17 (ESV) says, "Thus says the LORD, your Redeemer, the Holy One of Israel: "I am the Lord your God, who teaches you to profit, who leads you by the way you should go". I'm assured in knowing that God desires to teach me how to live according to His principles. The word profit in this verse is not referring to material possessions, yet it refers to the things we need to live godly and holy before God, in order to be profitable in God. As it says in 2 Timothy 3:16 (NKJV "All Scripture *is* given by inspiration of God, and *is* profitable for doctrine, for reproof, for correction, for instruction in righteousness."

Secondly, God desires to lead me in the way I should go. Listen all of us come into this Christian journey with some idea where we desire to go and do. But what I've learned is that no matter what your agenda may be, when you're fully surrendered to God you learn that your will must be given up for His.

Not so you can be enslaved to Him.

But so you can be an honorable servant.

Knowing fully that you don't have to worry about where He leads because you know you will never regret leaning and trusting in Him

Wisdom Principle to Practice: Be determined to follow God with joy, even when you don't know where He's leading.

Notes

Day 30

Your Why Will Lead to Your What
(Deuteronomy 28:13)

"And the Lord will make you the head and not the tail, and you shall only go up and not down, if you obey the commandments of the Lord your God, which I command you today, being careful to do them." Deuteronomy 28:13 (ESV)

I remember growing up and greatly enjoying learning in English class. There was just something exciting to me in learning sentence structure, conjugating verbs, and just learning the importance of proper communication was extremely important to me. One of the lessons I learned and held dear was that of "cause and effect". The cause is the reason why something happens, and the effect is what happens because of the cause. For example, I did not study well for the exam, therefore I failed it or because the alarm was not set we were late for work. Cause and effect is a very powerful yet neglected principle that we fail to apply in life. Oftentimes we fall to pieces with questions and doubts instead of realizing, your "Why" always leads the way to your "What".

Unfortunately, as believers we consider the law of cause and effect when it comes to every aspect of our lives, except when it comes to our walk with God. We certainly do not consider the principle of cause and effect when it comes to receiving our promises or blessings from God. But as children of God we cannot negate that this principle is at work in our relationship with God.

In this twenty-first century, so many people want blessings from God without being accountable to God. They want God to do His part without making sure they are doing theirs. Many times you will hear people recite today's scripture as a declaration to validate who they are. You will hear people say, "I am the head and not the tail, I am above and not beneath". However, we must be careful and mindful not to lose the value or accountability of this scripture, by only reciting the first portion of the text. God made these pronouncements of blessings to the children of Israel and us contingent on one thing; if we obey His commandments.

We cannot rightly claim possession to the blessings and promises of God, without first committing to obey the Word of God. We cannot rightfully expect God to move on our behalf, or manifest the promises available to us, if we do not first meet the requirements for them to be fulfilled in our lives.

Being blessed, walking in your purpose and having a fruitful life is not given to us only because we belong to God, but because we are obedient to God.

So, remember, "Why" always leads to your "What".

Wisdom Principe to Practice: Don't just focus on "why" God is allowing something to happen in your life. Ask him to reveal to you "what" he is allowing it for.

Notes

www.ingramcontent.com/pod-product-compliance
Lightning Source LLC
Chambersburg PA
CBHW071154090426
42736CB00012B/2333